DO THE WORK!

Also by Steven Pressfield

FICTION

The Legend of Bagger Vance
Gates of Fire
Tides of War
Last of the Amazons
The Virtues of War
The Afghan Campaign
Killing Rommel
The Profession
The Knowledge
36 Righteous Men
A Man at Arms

NONFICTION

The War of Art
The Warrior Ethos
Turning Pro
The Authentic Swing
The Lion's Gate
An American Jew
*Nobody Wants to Read Your Sh*t*
The Artist's Journey
Put Your Ass Where Your Heart Wants to Be
Govt Cheese: A Memoir

DO THE WORK!

Overcome Resistance
and get out of your own way

By Steven Pressfield
Author of *The War of Art*

First Published in India

Sanage Publishing House

The Domino Project

Published by Do You Zoom, Inc. and Black Irish Entertainment LLC.

Sign up for updates and free stuff at www.thedominoproject.com.

LIBRARY OF CONGRESS CATALOGING IN PUBLICATION DATA

Pressfield, Steven, 1943—

Do The Work!: Overcome Resistance and get out of your own way / Steven Pressfield

p. cm.

ISBN 978-8-119216-39-0 (Paperback)
ISBN 978-8-119216-49-9 (Hardback)
ISBN 978-8-119216-43-7 (eBook)

DO THE WORK!

For Ellie

Foreword

Right there, in your driveway, is a really fast car. Not one of those stupid Hamptons-style, rich-guy, showy cars like a Ferrari, but an honest fast car, perhaps a Subaru WRX. And here are the keys. Now go drive it.

Right there, on the runway, is a private jet, ready to fly you wherever you want to go. Here's the pilot, standing by. Go. Leave.

Right there, in your hand, is a Chicago Pneumatics 0651 hammer. You can drive a nail through just about anything with it, again and again if you choose. Time to use it.

And here's a keyboard, connected to the entire world. Here's a publishing platform you can use to interact with just about anyone, just about any time, for free. You wanted a level playing field, one where you have just as good a shot as anyone else? Here it is. Do the work.

That's what we're all waiting for you to do—to do the work.

Steven Pressfield is the author of the most important book you've never read: *The War of Art*. It will help you understand why you're stuck, it will kick you in the pants, and it will get you moving. You should, no, you must buy a copy as soon as you finish reading this.

In this manifesto, Steve gets practical, direct, and personal. Read it fast; then read it again and take notes. Then buy a copy for everyone else who's stuck and push them to get to work as well.

Hurry.

Seth Godin
Hastings-on-Hudson, January 2011

A Note From The Author

In 2010, Amazon.com had an idea to publish books itself, in addition to providing a marketplace for the works of others. Amazon reached out to one of its favorite writers, the tech and internet visionary Seth Godin (*Tribes, Linchpin, Purple Cow*, many more). Seth said yes, let's do it.

Thus was born the Domino Project---a partnership between Amazon and Seth Godin.

Domino's first book was Seth's *Poke the Box*. *Poke the Box* was a short, brilliant book encouraging artists and entrepreneurs to be brave, to test their own limits and the limits of their talent.

Domino's second book was the one you're reading now. Seth invited me to contribute, based on our friendship (I've been a huge fan of Seth's for years) and the response to my own 2002 book on creativity, *The War of Art*.

As it turned out, I was working on a book right then that I thought would be perfect for Domino. It was a follow-up to *The War of Art* that I was calling *Do This!* The book took the principles of *The War of Art* and imagined a writer or artist or entrepreneur just as they were starting a new project ... at the moment when they found themselves peering fearfully into the mirror and asking themselves, "What the heck have I gotten myself into?"

In other words, when they first started experiencing their own Resistance---my term for the fear, self-doubt, tendency to procrastination, vulnerability to distraction, and just plain self-sabotage that strikes all of us at that fateful moment.

Do This!, in my mind, would be a working companion for this terror-stricken artist or entrepreneur. It would walk him or her through all the stages of a project, focusing on the predictable points (before we begin, after Act One, in the "deep middle," just before the end, and after we finish) when Resistance would strike most powerfully. *Do This!* would help the self-doubting artist work his or her way through these points to *finish the damn thing!*

I turned the manuscript in to Seth. He loved it but he hated the title. A week later I got an email from him. "How about *Do the Work*?"

I loved it.

And that's how this book came to be. I hope you like it. I hope it helps you on your project.

Good luck and *Do the Work*!

Steven Pressfield
May, 2023

On the field of the Self stand a knight and a dragon.

You are the knight. Resistance is the dragon.

About This Book

This book is designed to coach you through a project (a book, a ballet, a new business venture, a philanthropic enterprise) from conception to finished product, seeing it from the point of view of Resistance.

We'll hit every predictable Resistance Point along the way—those junctures where fear, self-sabotage, procrastination, self-doubt, and all those other demons we're all so familiar with can be counted upon to strike.

> Where butts need to be kicked, we shall kick them. Where kinder, gentler methods are called for, we'll get out the kid gloves.

One note: This document is articulated for the most part in the lexicon of a writer—i.e., the model used is that of conceiving and constructing plays, novels, or screenplays. But the principles can be applied with equal effectiveness to any form of creative endeavor, including such seemingly far-afield enterprises as the acquisition of physical fitness, the recovery from a broken heart, or the pursuit of any objective—emotional, intellectual, or spiritual—that involves moving from a lower or less conscious plane to a higher one.

ORIENTATION
ENEMIES AND ALLIES

Our Enemies

The following is a list of the forces arrayed against us as artists and entrepreneurs:

1. Resistance (i.e., fear, self-doubt, procrastination, addiction, distraction, timidity, ego and narcissism, self-loathing, perfectionism, etc.)
2. Rational thought
3. Friends and family

Resistance

What exactly is this monster? The following few chapters from *The War of Art* will bring us up to speed:

Resistance's Greatest Hits

The following is a list, in no particular order, of those activities that most commonly elicit Resistance:

1. The pursuit of any calling in writing, painting, music, film, dance, or any creative art, however marginal or unconventional.
2. The launching of any entrepreneurial venture or enterprise, for profit or otherwise.
3. Any diet or health regimen.
4. Any program of spiritual advancement.

5. Any activity whose aim is the acquisition of chiseled abdominals.
6. Any course or program designed to overcome an unwholesome habit or addiction.
7. Education of every kind.
8. Any act of political, moral, or ethical courage, including the decision to change for the better some unworthy pattern of thought or conduct in ourselves.
9. The undertaking of any enterprise or endeavor whose aim is to help others.
10. Any act that entails commitment of the heart—the decision to get married, to have a child, to weather a rocky patch in a relationship.
11. The taking of any principled stand in the face of adversity.

In other words, any act that rejects immediate gratification in favor of long-term growth, health, or integrity.

Or, expressed another way, any act that derives from our higher nature instead of our lower. Any of these acts will elicit Resistance.

Now: what are the characteristics of Resistance?

Resistance Is Invisible

Resistance cannot be seen, heard, touched, or smelled. But it can be felt. We experience it as an energy field radiating from a work-in-potential.

Resistance is a repelling force. It's negative. Its aim is to shove us away, distract us, prevent us from doing our work.

Resistance Is Insidious

Resistance will tell you anything to keep you from doing your work. It will perjure, fabricate, falsify; seduce, bully, cajole. Resistance is protean. It will assume any form, if that's what it takes to deceive you.

Resistance will reason with you like a lawyer or jam a nine-millimeter in your face like a stickup man.

Resistance has no conscience. It will pledge anything to get a deal, then double-cross you as soon as your back is turned. If you take Resistance at its word, you deserve everything you get.

Resistance is always lying and always full of shit.

Resistance Is Impersonal

Resistance is not out to get you personally. It doesn't know who you are and doesn't care. Resistance is a force of nature. It acts objectively.

Though it feels malevolent, Resistance in fact operates with the indifference of rain and transits the heavens by the same laws as stars. When we marshal our forces to combat Resistance, we must remember this.

Resistance Is Infallible

Like a magnetized needle floating on a surface of oil, Resistance will unfailingly point to true North—meaning that calling or action it most wants to stop us from doing.

We can use this.

We can use it as a compass.

We can navigate by Resistance, letting it guide us to that calling or purpose that we must follow before all others.

Rule of thumb: The more important a call or action is to our soul's evolution, the more Resistance we will feel toward pursuing it.

Resistance Is Universal

We're wrong if we think we're the only ones struggling with Resistance. Everyone who has a body experiences Resistance.

Resistance Never Sleeps

Henry Fonda was still throwing up before each stage performance, even when he was seventy-five.

In other words, fear doesn't go away. The warrior and the artist live by the same code of necessity, which dictates that the battle must be fought anew every day.

Resistance Plays for Keeps

Resistance's goal is not to wound or disable.

Resistance aims to kill.

Its target is the epicenter of our being: our genius, our soul, the unique and priceless gift we were put on this earth to give and that no one else has but us. Resistance means business.

When we fight it, we are in a war to the death.

Rational Thought

Next to Resistance, rational thought is the artist or entrepreneur's worst enemy.

Bad things happen when we employ rational thought, because rational thought comes from the ego.

Instead, we want to work from the Self, that is, from instinct and intuition, from the unconscious.

Homer began both *The Iliad* and *The Odyssey* with a prayer to the Muse. The Greeks' greatest poet understood that genius did not reside within his fallible, mortal self—but came to him instead from some source that he could neither command nor control, only invoke.

When an artist says "Trust the soup," she means let go of the need to control (which we can't do anyway) and put your faith instead in the Source, the Mystery, the Quantum Soup.

The deeper the source we work from, the better our stuff will be—and the more transformative it will be for us and for those we share it with.

Friends and Family

The problem with friends and family is that they know us *as we are*. They are invested in maintaining us as we are.

The last thing we want is to remain as we are.

If you're reading this book, it's because you sense inside you a second self, an unlived you.

With some exceptions (God bless them), friends and family are the enemy of this unmanifested you, this unborn self, this future being.

Prepare yourself to make new friends. They will appear, trust me.

Our Allies

Enough for now about the antagonists arrayed against us. Let's consider the champions on our side:

1. Stupidity
2. Stubbornness
3. Blind faith
4. Passion
5. Assistance (the opposite of Resistance)
6. Friends and family

Stay Stupid

The three dumbest guys I can think of: Charles Lindbergh, Steve Jobs, Winston Churchill. Why? Because any smart person who understood how impossibly arduous were the tasks they had set themselves would have pulled the plug before he even began.

Ignorance and arrogance are the artist and entrepreneur's indispensable allies. She must be clueless enough to have no idea how difficult her enterprise is going to be—and cocky enough to believe she can pull it off anyway.

How do we achieve this state of mind? By staying stupid. By not allowing ourselves to think.

A child has no trouble believing the unbelievable, nor does the genius or the madman. It's only you and I, with our big brains and our tiny hearts, who doubt and overthink and hesitate.

Don't think. Act.

We can always revise and revisit once we've acted. But we can accomplish nothing until we act.

Be Stubborn

Once we commit to action, the worst thing we can do is to stop.

What will keep us from stopping? Plain old stubbornness.

I like the idea of stubbornness because it's less lofty than "tenacity" or "perseverance." We don't have to be heroes to be stubborn. We can just be pains in the butt.

When we're stubborn, there's no quit in us. We're mean. We're mulish. We're ornery.

We're in till the finish.

We will sink our junkyard-dog teeth into Resistance's ass and not let go, no matter how hard he kicks.

Blind Faith

Is there a spiritual element to creativity? Hell, yes.

Our mightiest ally (our indispensable ally) is belief in something we cannot see, hear, touch, taste, or feel.

Resistance wants to rattle that faith. Resistance wants to destroy it.

There's an exercise that Patricia Ryan Madson describes in her wonderful book, *Improv Wisdom*. (Ms. Madson taught improvisational theater at Stanford to standing-room only classes for twenty years.) Here's the exercise:

Imagine a box with a lid. Hold the box in your hand. Now open it.

What's inside?

It might be a frog, a silk scarf, a gold coin of Persia. But here's the trick: no matter how many times you open the box, there is always something in it.

Ask me my religion. That's it.

I believe with unshakeable faith that there will always be something in the box.

Passion

Picasso painted with passion, Mozart composed with it. A child plays with it all day long.

You may think that you've lost your passion, or that you can't identify it, or that you have so much of it, it threatens to overwhelm you. None of these is true.

Fear saps passion.

When we conquer our fears, we discover a boundless, bottomless, inexhaustible well of passion.

Assistance

We'll come back to this later. Suffice it to say for now that as Resistance is the shadow, its opposite—Assistance—is the sun.

Friends and Family

When art and inspiration and success and fame and money have come and gone, who still loves us—and whom do we love?

> Only two things will remain with us across the river: our inhering genius and the hearts we love.

In other words, what we do and whom we do it for.

But enough theory. In the next chapter we'll start our novel, kick off our new business, launch our philanthropic enterprise.

First question: When is the best time to start?

1 BEGINNING

Start Before You're Ready

Don't prepare. Begin.

> Remember, our enemy is not lack of preparation; it's not the difficulty of the project or the state of the marketplace or the emptiness of our bank account.

The enemy is Resistance.

> The enemy is our chattering brain, which, if we give it so much as a nanosecond, will start producing excuses, alibis, transparent self-justifications, and a million reasons why we can't/shouldn't/won't do what we know we need to do.

Start before you're ready.

Good things happen when we start before we're ready. For one thing, we show *huevos*. Our blood heats up. Courage begets more courage. The gods, witnessing our boldness, look on in approval. W. H. Murray said:

> Until one is committed, there is hesitancy, the chance to draw back, always ineffectiveness. Concerning all acts of initiative (and creation), there is one elementary truth, the ignorance of which kills countless ideas and splendid plans: that the moment one definitely commits oneself, then Providence moves too. A whole stream of events issues from the decision, raising in one's favor all manner of unforeseen incidents and meetings and material assistance which no man could have dreamed would have come his way. I have learned a deep respect for one of Goethe's couplets: "Whatever you can do or dream you can, begin it. Boldness has genius, power and magic in it." Begin it now.

A Research Diet

Before we begin, you wanna do research? Uh-unh. I'm putting you on a diet.

> You're allowed to read three books on your subject. No more.

No underlining, no highlighting, no thinking or talking about the documents later. Let the ideas percolate.

> Let the unconscious do its work.

Research can become Resistance. We want to work, not prepare to work.

(Later we'll come back and do serious, heavy-duty research. Later. Not now.)

Two quick thoughts as we begin:

1. Stay Primitive

The creative act is primitive. Its principles are of birth and genesis.

> Babies are born in blood and chaos; stars and galaxies come into being amid the release of massive primordial cataclysms.

Conception occurs at the primal level. I'm not being facetious when I stress, throughout this book, that it is better to be primitive than to be sophisticated, and better to be stupid than to be smart.

> The most highly cultured mother gives birth sweating and dislocated and cursing like a sailor.

That's the place we inhabit as artists and innovators. It's the place we must become comfortable with.

> The hospital room may be spotless and sterile, but birth itself will always take place amid chaos, pain, and blood.

2. Swing for the Seats

My first job was in advertising in New York. I used to bring ideas to my boss that were so tiny, they made him apoplectic.

> "This idea is the size of a postage stamp! If it were any more miniscule, I'd need an electron microscope just to see it! Go back to your cubicle and bring me something BIG!"

If you and I want to do great stuff, we can't let ourselves work small. A home-run swing that results in a strikeout is better than a successful bunt or even a line-drive single.

Start playing from power. We can always dial it back later. If we don't swing for the seats from the start, we'll never be able to drive a fastball into the upper deck.

Lunch with My Mentor

Some years ago I had lunch at Joe Allen's in Manhattan with my mentor (though he would cringe at that word), the writer and documentary maker Norm Stahl. He was making some notes on a pad of yellow, legal-size foolscap paper. He told me something that has saved my bacon more times than I can count:

> Steve, God made a single sheet of yellow foolscap exactly the right length to hold the outline of an entire novel.

What did Norm mean by that?

He meant don't overthink. Don't overprepare. Don't let research become Resistance. Don't spend six months compiling a thousand-page tome detailing the emotional matrix and family history of every character in your book.

Outline it fast. Now. On instinct.

Discipline yourself to boil down your story/new business/philanthropic enterprise to a single page.

Is this easy? Hell, no.

So the next chapter offers a helpful hint:

Three-Act Structure

Break the sheet of foolscap into three parts: beginning, middle, and end.

This is how screenwriters and playwrights work. Act One, Act Two, Act Three.

How Leonardo Did It

Here's the Last Supper in three acts on a single sheet of foolscap:

1. Supper table stretching across the width of the canvas.
2. Jesus standing in the center, apostles arrayed in various postures left and right.
3. Perspective and background tailing off behind.

That's all Mr. Da V needed to start. The rest is details.

Positively Fourth Street in Three Acts

1. "You got a lotta nerve to say you are my friend ....
2. " ... when you know as well as me, you'd rather see me paralyzed ...
3. " ... you'd know what a drag it is to see you."

The Vietnam Memorial

In three acts, on one sheet of foolscap:

1. A wall with the names of the fallen in chronological order of the dates of their deaths.
2. Wall set below the level of the ground in a "V," extending from a shallow end to a deep end.
3. Visitors descend to view the wall, which has no barrier to prevent them from touching the names of the memorialized or from leaving tokens of love or honor at the base of the wall.

At the conception stage, the artist works by instinct. What feels right?

What does she love?

Is this her pure vision? Does it feel so right to her that she can dedicate the next X years of her life to realizing it?

Those were the only questions, at the start, that Maya Lin needed to ask and answer.

Did she analyze her design intellectually? No doubt. Did she reflect on the utility of negative space and the power of what's-left-out? Of course. Did she assess with her intellect which aspects of the design would produce emotion and why? I'm sure she did.

But all that is beside the point at this stage. Let the art historians worry about that later.

> Do you love your idea? Does it feel right on instinct? Are you willing to bleed for it?

Facebook in Three Acts

1. A digital commons, upon which anyone who wishes may establish, free, his or her own personal "page."
2. Each page owner determines who is permitted access to his or her page.
3. Thus creating a worldwide community of "friends" who can interact with other "friends" and communicate or share virtually anything they want.

That's Why They Call It Rewriting

The old saw says there's no such thing as writing, only rewriting. This is true.

Better to have written a lousy ballet than to have composed no ballet at all.

> Get your idea down on paper. You can always tweak it later.

Next question: How do you get it down?

Start at the End

Here's a trick that screenwriters use: work backwards. Begin at the finish.

If you're writing a movie, solve the climax first. If you're opening a restaurant, begin with the experience you want the diner to have when she walks in and enjoys a meal. If you're preparing a seduction, determine the state of mind you want the process of romancing to bring your lover to.

> Figure out where you want to go; then work backwards from there.

Yes, you say. "But how do I know where I want to go?"

Answer the Question "What Is This About?"

Start with the theme. What is this project about?

What is the Eiffel Tower about?
What is the space shuttle about?
What is *Nude Descending a Staircase* about?

Your movie, your album, your new startup ... what is it about? When you know that, you'll know the end state. And when you know the end state, you'll know the steps to take to get there.

Moby Dick on a Single Sheet, Working Back to Front

What is *Moby Dick* about?

It's about the clash between human will and the elemental malice of nature, i.e. (in Melville's dark 19th-century view), the Old Testament God.

So ... a monster. A whale. A white whale (because white is even weirder and scarier than whatever color whales normally are).

Next: a mortal to challenge the monster. He must be monstrous himself. Obsessed, arrogant, monomaniacal. Ahab.

Knowing our theme (in other words, what *Moby Dick* is about), we now know the climax: Ahab harpoons the white whale and duels it to the death. No other climax is possible.

Now we have Act Three. We have our end.

Next: beginning and middle. We need to set the climax up and load it with maximum emotion and thematic impact.

We must, in other words, establish both protagonist and antagonist, make clear to the reader what each of them represents and what their conflict means thematically in the broader scheme of the human (and divine) condition.

Beginning: Ishmael. Our point of view. A human-scale witness to the tragedy.

Once we have Ishmael, we have our start and our ultimate finish—after the whale destroys the *Pequod* and all her crew and drags Ahab to his death in the depths, Ishmael pops up amid the wreckage, the lone survivor, to tell the tale.

> End first, then beginning and middle. That's your startup, that's your plan for competing in a triathlon, that's your ballet.

"But hey, Steve ... I thought you said 'Don't think.'"

Let's pause for a moment then and consider the difference between thinking and "thinking."

Thoughts and Chatter

Have you ever meditated? Then you know what it feels like to shift your consciousness to a witnessing mode and to watch thoughts arise, float across your awareness, and then drift away, to be replaced by the next thought and the thought after that.

These are not thoughts.
They are chatter.

I was thirty years old before I had an actual thought. Everything up till then was either what Buddhists call "monkey-mind" chatter or the reflexive regurgitation of whatever my parents or teachers said, or whatever I saw on the news or read in a book, or heard somebody rap about, hanging around the street corner.

In this book, when I say "Don't think," what I mean is: don't listen to the chatter. Pay no attention to those rambling, disjointed images and notions that drift across the movie screen of your mind.

Those are not your thoughts.

They are chatter.
They are Resistance.

Chatter is your mother and father's well-intentioned expressions of caution, seeking to shield you from hurting yourself. Chatter is your teachers' equally well-meaning attempts at socialization, training you to follow the rules. Chatter is your friends' regular-Joe buddy-talk, trying to make you like them and follow the rules of the pack.

Chatter is Resistance.

Its aim is to reconcile you to "the way it is," to make you exactly like everyone else, to render you amenable to societal order and discipline.

Where do our own real thoughts come from? How can we access them? From what source does our true, authentic self speak?

Answering that is the work you and I will do for the rest of our lives.

Ready to Rock and Roll

We've got our concept, we've got our theme. We know our start. We know where we want to finish. We've got our project in three acts on a single sheet of foolscap.

Ready to roll? We need only to remember our three mantras:

1. Stay primitive.
2. Trust the soup.
3. Swing for the seats.

And our final-final precept:

4. Be ready for Resistance.

MIDDLE

The Universe Is Not Indifferent

I blame Communism. I blame Fascism. I blame psychotherapy. They—and a boatload of other well-intentioned ideologies that evolved during the mass-culture, industrialized, dehumanizing epoch of the late 19th and early 20th centuries—all posited the same fantasy. They all preached that human nature was perfectible and that, thereby, evil could be overcome.

It can't.

When you and I set out to create anything—art, commerce, science, love—or to advance in the direction of a higher, nobler version of ourselves, we uncork from the universe, ineluctably, an equal and opposite reaction.

That reaction is Resistance. Resistance is an active, intelligent, protean, malign force—tireless, relentless, and inextinguishable—whose sole object is to stop us from becoming our best selves and from achieving our higher goals.

The universe is not indifferent. It is actively hostile.

Every principle espoused so far in this volume is predicated upon that truth. The aim of every axiom set forth thus far is to outwit, outflank, outmaneuver Resistance.

> We can never eliminate Resistance. It will never go away. But we can outsmart it, and we can enlist allies that are as powerful as it is.

One thing we can never, never permit ourselves to do is to take Resistance lightly, to underestimate it or to fail to take it into account.

We must respect Resistance, like Sigourney Weaver respected the Alien, or St. George respected the dragon.

Fill in the Gaps

On our single sheet of foolscap we've got the Big Beats. Now what?

Fill in the gaps.

David Lean famously declared that a feature film should have seven or eight major sequences. That's a pretty good guideline for our play, our album, our State of the Union address.

A video game should have seven or eight major movements; so should the newest high-tech gadget, or the latest fighter plane. Our new house should have seven or eight major spaces. A football game, a prize fight, a tennis match—if they're going to be entertaining—should have seven or eight major swings of momentum.

That's what we need now. We need to fill in the gaps with a series of great entertaining and enlightening scenes, sequences, or spaces.

Do Research Now

Now you can do your research. But stay on your diet.

Do research early or late. Don't stop working. Never do research in prime working time.

> Research can be fun. It can be seductive. That's its danger. We need it, we love it. But we must never forget that research can become Resistance.

Soak up what you need to fill in the gaps. Keep working.

How Screenwriters Pitch

When movie writers pitch a project, they keep it brief because studio executives' attention spans are minimal. But they, the writers, want their presentation to have maximum impact and to deliver, in concise form, the feel and flavor of the film they see in their heads.

One trick they use is to boil down their presentation to the following:

1. A killer opening scene
2. Two major set pieces in the middle
3. A killer climax
4. A concise statement of the theme

In other words, they're filling in the gaps. The major beats.

We can do that, too.

If we're inventing Twitter, we start with What Are You Doing Now?, the 140-character limit, and the Following. We fill in the gaps: the hashtag, the tiny URL, the re-tweet.

If we're writing *The Hangover*, we kick off with Losing Doug, Searching for Doug, Finding Doug. Fill in the blanks: Stu marries a stripper, Mike Tyson comes after his tiger, Mister Chow brings the muscle.

Any project or enterprise can be broken down into beginning, middle, and end. Fill in the gaps; then fill in the gaps between the gaps.

When we've got David Lean's eight sequences, we're home except for one thing:

The actual work.

Cover the Canvas

One rule for first full working drafts: get them done ASAP.

Don't worry about quality. Act, don't reflect. Momentum is everything.

Get to THE END as if the devil himself were breathing down your neck and poking you in the butt with his pitchfork.

Believe me, he is.

Get the serum to Nome. Get the Conestoga wagon to the Oregon Trail. Get the first version of your project done from A to Z as fast as you can.

> Don't stop. Don't look down.
> Don't think.

Suspend All Self-Judgment

Unless you're building a sailboat or the Taj Mahal, I give you a free pass to screw up as much as you like.

> The inner critic? His ass is not permitted in the building.

Set forth without fear and without self-censorship. When you hear that voice in your head, blow it off.

> This draft is not being graded.
> There will be no pop quiz.

Only one thing matters in this initial draft: get SOMETHING done, however flawed or imperfect.

> You are not allowed to judge yourself.

The Crazier the Better

My friend Paul is writing a cop novel. He's never written anything so ambitious—and he's terrified. "The story is coming out dark," he says. "I mean twisted, weird-dark. So dark it's scaring me."

Paul wants to know if he should throttle back. He's worried that the book will come out so evil, not even Darth Vader will want to touch it.

Answer: No way.

The darker the better, if that's how it's coming to him.

Suspending self-judgment doesn't just mean blowing off the "You suck" voice in our heads. It also means liberating ourselves from conventional expectations—from what we think our work "ought" to be or "should" look like.

Stay stupid. Follow your unconventional, crazy heart.

If your notion violates every precept I've set forth in these pages, tell me to go to hell. Do what that voice says.

Ideas Do Not Come Linearly

Remember when we broke our concept down into beginning, middle, and end? Rational thought would tempt us to do our work in that order.

Wrong.

> Ideas come according to their own logic. That logic is not rational. It's not linear. We may get the middle before we get the end. We may get the end before we get the beginning. Be ready for this. Don't resist it.

Do you have a pocket tape recorder? I do. I keep it with me everywhere. (A notepad works, too.) Why do I record ideas the minute they come to me? Because if I don't, I'll forget them. You will, too.

> Nothing is more fun than turning on the recorder and hearing your own voice telling you a fantastic idea that you had completely forgotten you had.

The Process

Let's talk about the actual process—the writing/composing/idea generation process.

It progresses in two stages: action and reflection.

Act, reflect. Act, reflect.

NEVER act and reflect at the same time.

The Definition of Action and Reflection

In writing, "action" means putting words on paper.

"Reflection" means evaluating what we have on paper.

For this first draft, we'll go light on reflection and heavy on action.

Spew. Let 'er rip. Launch into the void and soar wherever the wind takes you.

When we say "Trust the soup," we mean the Muse, the unconscious, the Quantum Soup. The sailor hoists his canvas, trusting that the wind (which is invisible and which he can neither see nor control) will appear and power him upon his voyage.

You and I hoist our canvas to catch ideas.

When we say "Stay Stupid," we mean don't self-censor, don't indulge in self-doubt, don't permit self-judgment.

Forget rational thought. Play. Play like a child.

Why does this purely instinctive, intuitive method work? Because our idea (our song, our ballet, our new Tex-Mex restaurant) is smarter than we are.

Our job is not to control our idea; our job is to figure out what our idea is (and wants to be)—and then bring it into being.

The song we're composing already exists in potential. Our work is to find it. Can we hear it in our head? It exists, like a signal coming from a faraway radio tower.

Our job is to tune to that frequency.

Did you read Bob Dylan's *Chronicles*? The lengths he goes to to find a song (or an arrangement or a producing partner) are beyond insanity.

He does it all by instinct. Fearless, child-like, primitive instinct.

The Answer Is Always Yes

When an idea pops into our head and we think, "No, this is too crazy,"

... that's the idea we want.

When we think, "This notion is completely off the wall ... should I even take the time to work on this?"

... the answer is yes.

Never doubt the soup. Never say no.

The answer is always yes.

The Opposite of Resistance

I said a few chapters ago that the universe is not indifferent; it is actively hostile. This is true.

But behind every law of nature stands an equal and opposite law.

The universe is also actively benevolent. You should be feeling this now. You should be feeling a tailwind.

The opposite of Resistance is Assistance.

A work-in-progress generates its own energy field. You, the artist or entrepreneur, are pouring love into the work; you are suffusing it with passion and intention and hope. This is serious juju. The universe responds to this. It has no choice.

Your work-in-progress produces its own gravitational field, created by your will and your attention. This field attracts like-spirited entities into its orbit.

What entities?

Ideas.

You started with a few scraps of a song; now you've got half an opera. You began with the crazy notion to restore a neglected park; now the lot is cleared and you've got volunteers tweeting and phoning at all hours. Your will and vision initiated the process, but now the process has acquired a life and momentum of its own.

The un-indifferent universe has stepped in to counter Resistance. It has introduced a positive opposing force.

Assistance is the universal, immutable force of creative manifestation, whose role since the Big Bang has been to translate potential into being, to convert dreams into reality.

Keep Working

Stephen King has confessed that he works every day. Fourth of July, his birthday, Christmas.

I love that. Particularly at this stage—what Seth Godin calls "thrashing" (a very evocative term)—momentum is everything. Keep it going.

How much time can you spare each day?

For that interval, close the door and—short of a family emergency or the outbreak of World War III—don't let ANYBODY in.

Keep working. Keep working.
Keep working.

Keep Working, Part Two

Sometimes on Wednesday I'll read something that I wrote on Tuesday and I'll think, "This is crap. I hate it and I hate myself." Then I'll re-read the identical passage on Thursday. To my astonishment, it has become brilliant overnight.

Ignore false negatives. Ignore false positives. Both are Resistance.

Keep working.

Keep Working, Part Three

Did I forget to say?

Keep working.

Act/Reflect, Part Two

Until now, our motto has been "Act, Don't Reflect." Now we revisit that notion.

Now that we're rolling, we can start engaging the left brain as well as the right. Act, then reflect. Act, then reflect.

Here's how I do it:

At least twice a week, I pause in the rush of work and have a meeting with myself. (If I were part of a team, I'd call a team meeting.)

I ask myself, again, of the project: "What is this damn thing about?"

Keep refining your understanding of the theme; keep narrowing it down.

This is the thorniest nut of any creative endeavor—and the one that evokes the fiercest Resistance.

It is pure hell to answer this question.

More books, movies, new businesses, etc. get screwed up (or rather, screw themselves up) due to failure to confront and solve this issue than for any other reason. It is make-or-break, do-or-die.

Paddy Chayefsky famously said, "As soon as I figure out the theme of my play, I write it down on a thin strip of paper and Scotch-tape it to the front of my typewriter. After that, nothing goes into that play that isn't on-theme."

Have that meeting twice a week. Pause and reflect. "What is this project about?" "What is its theme?" "Is every element serving that theme?"

Fill in the Gaps, Part Two

Ask yourself, "What's missing?"

Then fill that gap.

What's missing in the menu of your new restaurant? What have we left out in planning our youth center in the slums of São Paulo?

Did you ever see the movie *True Confessions*, starring Robert Duvall and Robert De Niro? The story is set in 1940s Los Angeles; De Niro is a rising-star monsignor for the L.A. diocese; Duvall plays his brother, a homicide detective investigating a Black Dahlia–type murder.

The script was great, the direction was tremendous. But in mid-shoot, De Niro's instincts told him something was missing. The audience had seen his character wheeling and dealing on behalf of the Church, hosting big-money fundraisers, getting schools built, playing golf with L.A. heavyweights.

De Niro went to Ulu Grosbard, the director, and asked for a scene where the audience gets to see where his character sleeps. Sounds crazy, doesn't it?

The result was a simple sequence, without dialogue, of De Niro's monsignor returning home in the evening to the dormitory (a former mansion) he shares with other senior priests of the diocese. He mounts the stairs alone, enters a room so bare it contains nothing but a bed, a chair, and an armoire, all looking like they came from the Goodwill store. De Niro's character takes off the cardigan sweater he is wearing and hangs it on a wire hanger in the armoire, which contains only one other shirt and a single pair of trousers. Then he sits on the bed. That's it. But in that one moment, we, the audience, see the character's entire life.

Ask yourself what's missing. Then fill that void.

Now We're Rolling

We're weeks into the project now. Good things are happening. We've established habit and rhythm. We've achieved momentum.

Ideas are flowing. Our movie, our new business, our passage to freedom from addiction has acquired gravitational mass; it possesses energy; its field produces attraction. The law of self-ordering has kicked in. Despite all our self-doubt, the project is rounding into shape. It's becoming itself.

People are responding to us differently. We're making new friends. Our feet are under us; we're starting to feel professional. We're beginning to feel as if we know a secret that nobody else does. Or rather, that we've somehow become part of a select society. Other members recognize us and encourage us; unsolicited, they proffer assistance—and their aid, unfailingly, is exactly what we've needed.

Best of all, we're having fun. The dread that had hamstrung us for years seems miraculously to have fallen away. The fog has lifted. It's almost too good to be true.

And then ...

The Wall

And then we hit the wall.

Out of nowhere, terror strikes. Our fragile confidence collapses. Nighttime: we wake in a sweat.

That "You suck" voice is back, howling in our head.

Did we stand up to someone in authority over us? Now we crawl back and grovel to him. Did we face up to someone who was treating us with disrespect? Now we beg him without shame to take us back.

We're poised at the brink of a creative breakthrough and we can't stand it. The prospect of success looms. We freak. Why did we start this project? We must have been insane. Who encouraged us? We want to wring their necks. Where are they now? Why can't they help us?

We're halfway, two-thirds through. Far enough to have invested serious time and money, not to mention our hopes, our dreams, our identity even—but not far enough to have passed the crisis point, not far enough to glimpse the end.

We have turned round Cape Horn and the gales are shrieking; ice encases the masts; sails and sheets are frozen. The storm howls dead in our faces. There's no way back and no way forward.

We know we're panicking but we can't stop; we can't get a hold of ourselves. We have entered ...

THE

BELLY

OF

THE

BEAST

Welcome to Hell

Now you're in the shit.

Now you're feeling the symptoms. Now you're ready to listen.

The next ten chapters are the most important in this book.

They're the movie within the movie, the dance within the dance. If you take away nothing else from this document, take this section.

It delineates the Seven Principles of Resistance and the two Tests.

These principles govern and underlie everything you're experiencing now. These tests are being set for you.

This is your trial by fire.

What follows is what you need to know to get to the other side.

Principle Number One: There Is an Enemy

The first principle of Resistance is that there is an enemy.

In our feel-good, social-safety-net, high-self-esteem world, you and I have been brainwashed to believe that there is no such thing as evil, that human nature is perfectible, that everyone and everything can be made nice.

We have been conditioned to imagine that the darkness that we see in the world and feel in our own hearts is only an illusion, which can be dispelled by the proper care, the proper love, the proper education, and the proper funding.

It can't.

There is an enemy. There is an intelligent, active, malign force working against us.

Step one is to recognize this.

This recognition alone is enormously powerful. It saved my life, and it will save yours.

Principle Number Two: This Enemy Is Implacable

The hostile, malicious force that we're experiencing now is not a joke. It is not to be trifled with or taken lightly. It is for real. In the words of my dear friend Rabbi Mordecai Finley:

"It will kill you. It will kill you like cancer."

This enemy is intelligent, protean, implacable, inextinguishable, and utterly ruthless and destructive.

Its aim is not to obstruct or to hamper or to impede.
Its aim is to kill.

This is the second principle of Resistance.

Principle Number Three: This Enemy Is Inside You

Pat Riley, when he was coach of the Lakers, had a term for all those off-court forces, like fame and ego (not to mention crazed fans, the press, agents, sponsors, and ex-wives), that worked against the players' chances for on-court success. He called these forces "peripheral opponents."

Resistance is not a peripheral opponent. It does not arise from rivals, bosses, spouses, children, terrorists, lobbyists, or political adversaries.

It comes from us.

You can board a spaceship to Pluto and settle, all by yourself, into a perfect artist's cottage ten zillion miles from Earth. Resistance will still be with you.

The enemy is inside you.

Principle Number Four: The Enemy Is Inside You, But It Is Not You

The fourth axiom of Resistance is that the enemy is inside you, but it is not you.

What does that mean? It means you are not to blame for the voices of Resistance you hear in your head.

They are not your "fault." You have done nothing "wrong." You have committed no "sin." I have that same voice in my head. So did Picasso and Einstein. So do Sarah Palin and Lady Gaga and Donald Trump.

If you've got a head, you've got a voice of Resistance inside it.

The enemy is in you, but it is not you. No moral judgment attaches to the possession of it. You "have" Resistance the same way you "have" a heartbeat.

You are blameless. You retain free will and the capacity to act.

Principle Number Five: The "Real You" Must Duel the "Resistance You"

On the field of the Self stand a knight and a dragon.

You are the knight. Resistance is the dragon.

There is no way to be nice to the dragon, or to reason with it or negotiate with it or beam a white light around it and make it your friend. The dragon belches fire and lives only to block you from reaching the gold of wisdom and freedom, which it has been charged to guard to its final breath.

The only intercourse possible between the knight and the dragon is battle.

The contest is life-and-death, *mano a mano*. It asks no quarter and gives none.

This is the fifth principle of Resistance.

Principle Number Six: Resistance Arises Second

The sixth principle of Resistance (and the key to overcoming it) is that Resistance arises second.

What comes first is the idea, the passion, the dream of the work we are so excited to create that it scares the hell out of us.

Resistance is the response of the frightened, petty, small-time ego to the brave, generous, magnificent impulse of the creative self.

Resistance is the shadow cast by the innovative self's sun.

What does this mean to us—the artists and entrepreneurs in the trenches?

It means that before the dragon of Resistance reared its ugly head and breathed fire into our faces, there existed within us a force so potent and life-affirming that it summoned this beast into being, perversely, to combat it.

It means that, at bottom, Resistance is not the towering, all-powerful monster before whom we are compelled to quake in terror. Resistance is more like the pain-in-the-ass schoolteacher who won't let us climb that tree in the playground.

But the urge to climb came first.

That urge is love.

Love for the material, love for the work, love for our brothers and sisters to whom we will offer our work as a gift.

In Greek, the word is *eros*. Life force. *Dynamis*, creative drive.

> That mischievous tree-climbing scamp is our friend.

She's us, she's our higher nature, our Self. In the face of Resistance, we have to remember her and hang onto her and draw strength from her.

> The opposite of fear is love—love of the challenge, love of the work, the pure joyous passion to take a shot at our dream and see if we can pull it off.

Principle Number Seven: The Opposite of Resistance Is Assistance

In myths and legends, the knight is always aided in his quest to slay the dragon. Providence brings forth a champion whose role is to assist the hero. Theseus had Ariadne when he fought the Minotaur. Jason had Medea when he went after the Golden Fleece. Odysseus had the goddess Athena to guide him home.

In Native American myths, our totemic ally is often an animal—a magic raven, say, or a talking coyote. In Norse myths, an old crone sometimes assists the hero; in African legends, it's often a bird. The three Wise Men were guided by a star.

All of these characters or forces represent Assistance. They are symbols for the unmanifested. They stand for a dream.

> The dream is your project, your vision, your symphony, your startup. The love is the passion and enthusiasm that fill your heart when you envision your project's completion.

Sometimes when Resistance is kicking my butt (which it does, all the time), I flash on Charles Lindbergh. What symphony of Resistance must have been playing in his head when he was struggling to raise the funding for his attempt to fly across the Atlantic solo?

"You're too young, you're too inexperienced; you've got no credentials, no credibility. Everyone who's tried this has failed and you will, too. It can't be done. Your plane will crash, you're going to drown, you're a madman who is attempting the impossible and you deserve whatever dire fate befalls you!"

What saw Lindy through?

It can only have been the dream.

Love of the idea.

How cool would it be, in 1927, to land at Le Bourget field outside Paris, having flown from New York, solo and non-stop, before anyone else had ever done it?

The seventh principle of Resistance is that we can align ourselves with these universal forces of Assistance—this dream, this passion to make the unmanifest manifest—and ride them into battle against the dragon.

Resistance's Two Tests

Resistance puts two questions to each and all of us.

Each question has only one correct answer.

Test Number One

"How bad do you want it?"

This is Resistance's first question. The scale below will help you answer. Mark the selection that corresponds to how you feel about your book/movie/ballet/new business/whatever.

Dabbling • Interested • Intrigued but Uncertain • Passionate • Totally Committed

If your answer is not the one on the far right, put this book down and throw it away.

Test Number Two

"Why do you want it?"

1. For the babes (or the dudes)
2. The money
3. For fame
4. Because I deserve it
5. For power

6. To prove my old man (or ex-spouse, mother, teacher, coach) wrong
7. To serve my vision of how life/mankind ought to be
8. For fun or beauty
9. Because I have no choice

If you checked 8 or 9, you get to stay on the island. (I know I said there was only one correct answer. But 8 and 9 are really one.)

If you checked any of the first seven, you can stay, too—but you must immediately check yourself into the Attitude Adjustment Chamber.

The Attitude Adjustment Chamber

Did you ever see *Cool Hand Luke*? Remember "the Box"? You don't get to keep anything when you enter this space. You must check at the door:

- Your ego
- Your sense of entitlement
- Your impatience
- Your fear
- Your hope
- Your anger

You must also leave behind:

- All grievances related to aspects of yourself dependent on the accident of birth, e.g., how neglected/abused/mistreated/unloved/poor/ill-favored etc. you were when you were born.
- All sense of personal exceptionalness dependent on the accident of birth, e.g., how rich/cute/tall/thin/smart/charming/loveable you were when you were born.
- All of the previous two, based on any subsequent (i.e., post-birth) acquisition of any of these qualities, however honorably or meritoriously earned.

The only items you get to keep are love for the work, will to finish, and passion to serve the ethical, creative Muse.

This ends our special section, "Belly of the Beast." We return now to programming already in progress:

You and me, two-thirds through our project and stuck in a hell of Resistance.

2
MIDDLE

The Big Crash

We were doing so great. Our project was in high gear, we were almost finished (maybe we actually were finished).

Then inevitably ...

Everything crashes.

If our project is a movie, the star checks into rehab. If it's a business venture, the bank pulls our financing. If it's a rodeo, our star bull runs away with a heifer.

The Big Crash is so predictable, across all fields of enterprise, that we can practically set our watches by it.

Bank on it. It's gonna happen.

The worst part of the Big Crash is that nothing can prepare us for it. Why? Because the crash arises organically, spawned by some act of commission or omission that we ourselves took or countenanced back at the project's inception.

The Big Crash just happened to me. My newest book, a novel called *The Profession*, was done—after two years of work. I was proud of it, I was psyched, I was sure I had broken through to a level I had never achieved before.

Then I showed it to people I trusted.

They hated it.

Let me rephrase that.

They HATED it.

The worst part is, they were right. The book didn't work. Its concept was flawed, and the flaw was fatal.

I'd love to report that I rallied at once and whipped that sucker into shape in a matter of days. Unfortunately, what happened was that I crashed just like the book.

I went into an emotional tailspin.
I was lost. I was floundering.

Ringing the Bell

Navy SEAL training puts its candidates through probably the most intense physical ordeal in the U.S. military. The reason is they're trying to break you. SEAL trainers want to see if the candidate will crack. Better that the aspiring warrior fails here—at Coronado Island in San Diego—than someplace where a real wartime mission and real lives are at stake.

In SEAL training, they have a bell. When a candidate can't take the agony any longer—the 6-mile ocean swims or the 15-mile full-load runs or the physical and mental ordeals on no sleep and no food ... when he's had enough and he's ready to quit, he walks up and rings the bell.

That's it. It's over.

He has dropped out.

You and I have a bell hanging over us, too, here in the belly of the beast. Will we ring it?

There's a difference between Navy SEAL training and what you and I are facing now.

Our ordeal is harder. Because we're alone.

We've got no trainers over us, shouting in our ears or kicking our butts to keep us going. We've got no friends, no fellow sufferers, no externally imposed structure. No one's feeding us, housing us, or clothing us. We have no objective milestones or points of validation. We can't tell whether we're doing great or falling on our faces. When we finish, if we do, no one will be waiting to congratulate us. We'll get no champagne, no beach party, no diploma, no insignia. The battle we're fighting, we can't explain to anybody or share with anybody or call in anybody to help.

The only thing we have in common with the SEAL candidates is the bell.

Will we ring it or won't we?

Crashes Are Good

Crashes are hell, but in the end they're good for us.

A crash means we have failed. We gave it everything we had and we came up short. A crash does not mean we are losers.

A crash means we have to grow.

A crash means we're at the threshold of learning something, which means we're getting better, we're acquiring the wisdom of our craft. A crash compels us to figure out what works and what doesn't work—and to understand the difference.

We got ourselves into this mess by mistakes we made at the start. How? Were we lazy? Inattentive? Did we mean well but forget to factor in human nature? Did we assess reality incorrectly?

Whatever the cause, the Big Crash compels us to go back now and solve the problem that we either created directly or set into motion unwittingly at the outset.

Sartre said "Hell is other people," but in this case, hell is us.

Panic Is Good

Creative panic is good. Here's why:

Our greatest fear is fear of success.

When we are succeeding—that is, when we have begun to overcome our self-doubt and self-sabotage, when we are advancing in our craft and evolving to a higher level—that's when panic strikes.

It did for me when my book crashed, and it was the best thing that happened to me all year.

When we experience panic, it means that we're about to cross a threshold. We're poised on the doorstep of a higher plane.

Have you ever watched a small child take a few bold steps away from its mother? The little boy or girl shows great courage. She ventures forth, feels exhilaration, and then ... she realizes what she has done. She freaks. She bolts back to Mommy.

That's you and me when we're growing.

Next time, the child won't run back to Mommy so fast. Next time, she'll venture farther.

Her panic was momentary, a natural part of the process of growth.

That's us as we rally and re-tackle the Big Crash. This time we'll lick it. We'll fix this jalopy and get it back on the road.

Panic is good. It's a sign that we're growing.

Back to Square One

In the belly of the beast, we go back to our allies:

- Stupidity
- Stubbornness
- Blind faith

We are too dumb to quit and too mulish to back off.

In the belly of the beast, we remind ourselves of two axioms:

1. The problem is not us. The problem is the problem.
2. Work the problem.

The Problem Is the Problem

A professional does not take success or failure personally. That's Priority Number One for us now.

> That our project has crashed is not a reflection of our worth as human beings. It's just a mistake. It's a problem—and a problem can be solved.

Now we go back to our sheet of yellow foolscap.

Where did we go wrong? Where did this train go off the tracks?

Somewhere in the three sections on our sheet of foolscap—beginning, middle, and end—and in the final section, the summation of the theme ... somewhere in there lies the answer. Why is it so hard to find? It's hard because it's hard.

I'm not trying to be cryptic or facetious. We went wrong at the start because the problem was so hard (and the act of solving it was so painful) that we ducked and dodged and bypassed. We hoped it would go away. We hoped it would solve itself. A little voice warned us then, but we were too smart to listen.

The bad news is, the problem is hell.

The good news is it's just a problem.

It's not us. We are not worthless or evil or crazy. We're just us, facing a problem.

Work the Problem

Here's what crashed in my book—and how I solved it:

The book, as I said, is called *The Profession*. It's a military/political thriller set a few years in the future, when mercenary armies have replaced conventional ones.

Scene after scene almost worked. But they all ran onto the same rocks: the events were so proximate time-wise that they could be doubted and second-guessed. The reader could say, "That's bullshit, I was there and it didn't happen like that." And the events were too emotionally charged (9/11 played a role and so did fictional withdrawals from Iraq and Afghanistan) and involved such painful real-world issues (did our troops die in vain?) that they overwhelmed the basically simple story and pulled it off its politically speculative-future theme.

Remember what we said before about friends and family? The answer came from there, from two people very close to me (they know who they are) who thrashed in and banged around inside the problem. They couldn't see the full solution, but the ideas that they stirred up helped me see it.

The answer was to move the book out farther into the future.

That was the stroke that split the diamond.

In other words, nothing mystical, nothing New Age-y, nothing involving the Law of Attraction.

The solution was mechanical.

It was like saying "Get the drive-wheel back on the pavement; then the car will come out of the ditch." Or "put the ship-date off one month to give us time to repair the glitches first."

It worked. It took an extra year, but it solved the problem.

And yes, the book did crash a second time after that, requiring a second trip back to Square One.

What else is new?

Moby Dick When It Crashes

Just for fun, let's imagine that *Moby Dick* crashed 9/10ths of the way through and Herman Melville texted us in a panic, pleading for help. What would the rescue operation look like?

We hurry over to HM's house and read the manuscript. Mel already has feedback from other friends and colleagues. All agree the book isn't working. We ask our Big Question: "What's missing?" The consensus focuses on the captain.

One comment: "He's kinda like Captain Queeg, an unbalanced neurotic." Another: "He reminded me of Captain Bligh—an autocratic prick."

Let's go to the foolscap. What does it say about the skipper?

> *Next: a mortal to challenge the monster. He must be monstrous himself. Obsessed, arrogant, monomaniacal. Ahab.*

Hmmm. Let's dig deeper. What does the foolscap say about the theme?

> *... the clash between human will and the elemental malice of nature.*

Melville is freaking a little; he's too close to the material, he has identified his hopes with it too much. Plus he's broke and the rent is due. We've given him a couple of stiff tots of rum; he's lying down in the bedroom. But still, the Problem. What exactly is it?

Two things.

First, Ahab as he stands now is weak; he's not a worthy opponent for the White Whale. We have to beef him up.

Second, the theme is incomplete.

Again we ask, "What's missing?"

Ahab needs to be more monstrous, more monomaniacal. How can we accomplish that?

1. Give him a peg leg. (Remember, this wasn't a cliché in the 1850s.)
2. Not just any peg leg, but one made of whale ivory.

3. Add that Ahab lost the leg, fighting a whale.
4. Not just any whale, but Moby Dick himself.
5. Let Ahab tramp the quarterdeck nightlong, obsessed with vengeance—and let the echo of that whale-ivory leg resound through the crew's quarters below like a knell of madness.
6. Add a crazed white streak running through Ahab's hair and beard, as if metaphysical hatred-lightning had carved a scar upon his soul.
7. Add beats to heighten Ahab's obsession. Here's one: When the *Pequod* passes another whaling vessel, the *Rachel*, which has just seen and fought Moby Dick and lost beloved members of the crew, including the captain's son, for whom they're searching now, let Ahab spurn all appeals for help and drive his own ship faster in pursuit of the white whale.
8. Let Ahab renounce his whaling contract and denounce the for-profit nature of the voyage. The hell with killing other whales for their oil! Ahab will hunt Moby Dick for vengeance alone!

These changes are helping. Ahab is much better than he was before, with two good legs and regular hair. But we need more.

We need to take the theme one level deeper ...

The story can't just be about "the clash between man's will and the malice of nature." That's not enough. It must add the element of man-as-part-of-nature-himself. So that Man is dueling the evil *inside himself* and being consumed by it.

Again, "What's missing?"

The involvement of the crew! If Ahab is the only crazy person aboard and the crew meekly follows him, that's no good. The men must become as obsessed as their captain.

A new scene. Ahab assembles the crew and forges new harpoons, made not for other whales but only to kill Moby Dick.

> "Advance, ye mates! Cross your lances full before me. Well done! Let me touch the axis." [Ahab pours the full voltage of his own electric hate, by the medium of his hand, into the lances of his three harpooneers.] "Drink, ye harpooneers! drink and swear ... Death to Moby Dick! God hunt us all, if we do not hunt Moby Dick to his death!"

That's Why They Call It Rewriting, Part Two

Does the prior Ahab scenario sound far-fetched? Melville was a genius, you say; he could never fail to realize a character to the fullest on his first try.

Maybe. Probably. But if this didn't happen to HM then, I promise you it happened to him other times. And it happened to a million other guys and gals, over and over and over.

No matter how great a writer, artist, or entrepreneur, he is a mortal, he is fallible. He is not proof against Resistance. He will drop the ball; he will crash.

That's why they call it rewriting.

The Point for Us

The point for you and me is that we have passed through hell. We have worked our problem.

We have solved it.

We have escaped from the belly of the beast.

END

Killer Instinct

Why does Seth Godin place so much emphasis on "shipping"?

Because finishing is the critical part of any project. If we can't finish, all our work is for nothing.

When we ship, we declare our stuff ready for prime time. We pack it in a FedEx box and send it out into the world. Our movie hits the screens, our smart phone arrives in the stores, our musical opens on Broadway.

It takes balls of steel to ship.

Here's a true nugget from *The War of Art:*

> I had a good friend who had labored for years and had produced an excellent and deeply personal novel. It was done. He had it in its mailing box, complete with cover letter to his agent. But he couldn't make himself send it off. Fear of rejection unmanned him.

Shipping is not for the squeamish or the faint of heart. It requires killer instinct. We've got the monster down; now we have to drive a stake through its heart.

Hamlet and Michael Crichton

How hard is it to finish something? The greatest drama in the English language was written on this very subject. Hamlet knows he must kill his uncle for murdering his father. But then he starts to think—and the next thing you know, the poor prince is so self-befuddled, he's ready to waste himself with a bare bodkin.

> Thus conscience does make cowards of us all,
>
> And thus the native hue of resolution
>
> Is sicklied o'er with the pale cast of thought,
>
> And enterprises of great pitch and moment
>
> With this regard their currents turn awry,
>
> And lose the name of action.

When Michael Crichton approached the end of a novel (so I've read), he used to start getting up earlier and earlier in the morning. He was desperate to keep his mojo going. He'd get up at six, then five, then three-thirty and two-thirty, till he was driving his wife insane.

Finally he had to move out of the house. He checked into a hotel (the Kona Village, which ain't so bad) and worked around the clock till he'd finished the book.

Michael Crichton was a pro.

He knew that Resistance was strongest at the finish. He did what he had to do, no matter how nutty or unorthodox, to finish and be ready to ship.

Fear of Success

I've never read anything better on the subject than this from Marianne Williamson:

> Our deepest fear is not that we are inadequate. Our deepest fear is that we are powerful beyond measure. It is our light, not our darkness, that most frightens us. We ask ourselves, Who am I to be brilliant, gorgeous, talented, fabulous? Actually, who are you not to be? You are a child of God. Your playing small does not serve the world. There is nothing enlightened about shrinking so that other people won't feel insecure around you. We are all meant to shine, as children do. We were born to make manifest the glory of God that is within us. It's not just in some of us; it's in everyone. And as we let our own light shine, we unconsciously give other people permission to do the same. As we are liberated from our own fear, our presence automatically liberates others.

Heaven and Books About Heaven

Have you seen this great New Yorker cartoon:

A perplexed person stands before two doors. One door says HEAVEN. The other says BOOKS ABOUT HEAVEN.

What makes us laugh, I suspect, is that all of us feel the pull to pick BOOKS ABOUT HEAVEN.

Are we that timid? Are our *huevos* that *pocito*?

When we're offered a chance at heaven, what diabolically craven force makes us want to back off—just for now, we promise ourselves—and choose instead heaven's pale reflection?

Fear of success is the essence of Resistance.

It's silent, covert, invisible ... but it permeates every aspect of our lives and poisons them in ways we're either blind to or in denial about.

In the belly of the beast,
you and I chose HEAVEN.
We've learned and we're stronger.
Now we face the final test.

Exposure

In mountaineering, there's a technical term called "exposure." A climber is exposed when there is nothing but thin air beneath her.

She can be a hundred feet from the summit of Everest and not be exposed, if there's a ledge or a shelf below. Conversely, she can be in shorts and a tank top down at the beach, practice-climbing on a boulder ten feet tall, and be completely exposed—if there's a fall beneath her.

When we ship, we're exposed.

That's why we're so afraid of it. When we ship, we'll be judged. The real world will pronounce upon our work and upon us. When we ship, we can fail. When we ship, we can be humiliated.

Here's another true story:

The first professional writing job I ever had, after seventeen years of trying, was on a movie called *King Kong Lives*. I and my partner-at-the-time, Ron Shusett (a brilliant writer and producer who also did *Alien* and *Total Recall*), hammered out the screenplay for Dino De Laurentiis. We were certain it was going to be a blockbuster. We invited everyone we knew to the premiere; we even rented out the joint next door for a post-triumph blowout.

Nobody showed. There was only one guy in line beside our guests, and he was muttering something about spare change. In the theater, our friends endured the movie in mute stupefaction. When the lights came up, they fled like cockroaches into the night.

Next day came the review in *Variety*:

> " ... Ronald Shusett and Steven Pressfield, we hope these are not their real names, for their parents' sake."

When the first week's grosses came in, the flick barely registered. Still I clung to hope. Maybe it's only tanking in urban areas; maybe it's playing better in the 'burbs. I motored to an Edge City multiplex. A youth manned the popcorn booth. "How's *King Kong Lives*?" I asked. He flashed thumbs-down. "Miss it, man. It sucks."

I was crushed.

I was forty-two years old, having given up everything normal in life to pursue the dream of being a writer; now I've finally got my name on a big-time Hollywood production starring Linda Hamilton, and what happens? I'm a loser, a phony; my life is worthless and so am I.

My friend Tony Keppelman snapped me out of it by asking if I was going to quit. Hell, no! "Then be happy," he said. "You're where you wanted to be, aren't you? So you're taking a few blows. That's the price for being in the arena and not on the sidelines. Stop complaining and be grateful."

That was when I realized I had become a pro. I had not yet had a success. But I had had a real failure.

When we ship, we open ourselves to judgment in the real world. Nothing is more empowering, because it plants us solidly on Planet Earth and gets us out of our self-devouring, navel-centered fantasies and self-delusions.

Ship it.

One Thing I Can Promise You

My personal *bête noire* of Resistance was shipping. When I was twenty-five, I had finished a novel 99.9 percent of the way. But I couldn't pull the trigger. I lost my nerve.

At that time, I had no idea there was such a thing as Resistance. I believed the voices in my head. I acted out. I blew up my marriage and blew up my life, rather than plunge a sword into the heart of that book and ship it.

It took me seven more years before I found the courage to face that dragon again—and another ten years after that before I had finally learned how to lay him out.

Here's one thing I can tell you—and you can take this to the bank:

Slay that dragon once, and he will never have power over you again.

Yeah, he'll still be there. Yeah, you'll still have to duel him every morning. And yeah, he'll still fight just as hard and use just as many nasty tricks as he ever did.

But you will have beaten him once, and you'll know you can beat him again. That's a game-changer. That will transform your life.

From the day I finally finished something, I've never had trouble finishing anything again.

I always deliver. I always ship.

Be Careful

Just because you've shipped doesn't mean Resistance is finished. Like the Terminator, it's morphing into an even crueler and more diabolical form. It'll be back.

This is a topic for another book: the level of maturity, professionalism, and personal involvement demanded by the tectonic overthrows happening today in positioning, branding, marketing—not to mention pure art and soul-authenticity. But that's for the future.

For now: congratulations!

You have done it!

Kudos to You

You've wrapped. You've shipped. You've licked this sonofabitch.

Kudos to you!

I salute anybody who took this vessel to sea and brought her safely again into port.

I stand in awe of anyone who hatches a dream and who shows the guts to hang tough, all alone, and see it through to reality.

I tip my hat to you for what you've done—for losing forty pounds, for kicking crack cocaine, for surviving the loss of someone you love, for facing any kind of adversity—internal or external—and slogging through. I come to attention when you walk past. I stand up for you like the spectators in the gallery stood up for Atticus Finch in *To Kill A Mockingbird*.

If no one has congratulated you, I do that now.

You have joined an elite fraternity, whether you realize it or not.

By dint of your efforts and your perseverance, you have initiated yourself into an invisible freemasonry whose members are awarded no badges or insignia, share no secret handshake, and wear no funny-looking hats.

But the fellows of this society recognize one another. I recognize you. I salute you.

You can be proud of yourself. You've done something that millions talk about but only a handful actually perform. And if you can do it once, you can do it again.

I don't care if you fail with this project. I don't care if you fail a thousand times.

You have done what only mothers and gods do: you have created new life.

Start (Again) Before You're Ready

I was living in a little town in northern California when I finally, after seventeen years of trying, finished my first novel. I drove over to my friend and mentor Paul Rink's house and told him what I had done. "Good for you," he said. "Now start the next one."

That's what I say now to you.

Take the rest of the day off. Take your wife or husband out to dinner. Pop some champagne. Give yourself a standing ovation.

Then get back to work. Begin the next one tomorrow.

Stay stupid.

Trust the soup.

Start before you're ready.

Acknowledgments

Thanks to Seth, Ishita, Willie, and Michael for being the brains behind this project. Thanks to Shawn and Callie for being my comrades in the trenches. Thanks to Amazon for supplying the muscle.

And thanks to you who've read this, for taking yourself (and us) forward.

About The Domino Project

Books worth buying are books worth sharing. We hope you'll find someone to give this copy to. You can find more about what we're up to at www.the-dominoproject.com.

Here are three ways you can spread the ideas in this manifesto:

1. Hold a discussion group in your office. Get people to read the book and come in and argue about it. How open is your company to innovation and failure? What will you do if your competitors get better at it than you are?
2. Give away copies. Lots of them. It turns out that when everyone in a group reads the same thing, conversations go differently.
3. Write the names of some of your peers on the inside back cover of this book (or scrawl them on a Post-it on your Kindle). As each person reads the book, have them scratch off their name and add someone else's.

We hope you'll share.

We are now faced with the fact, my friends, that tomorrow is today. We are confronted with the fierce urgency of now. In this unfolding conundrum of life and history, there is such a thing as being too late. Procrastination is still the thief of time. Life often leaves us standing bare, naked, and dejected with a lost opportunity. The tide in the affairs of men does not remain at flood—it ebbs. We may cry out desperately for time to pause in her passage, but time is adamant to every plea and rushes on. Over the bleached bones and jumbled residues of numerous civilizations are written the pathetic words, "Too late."

Martin Luther King, Jr.

Beyond Vietnam – A Time to Break Silence

New York City, April 4, 1967